X

Books by Ennis Rees:

Gillygaloos and Gollywhoppers

Pun Fun

Riddles, Riddles Everywhere

Tiny Tall Tales

Gillygaloos and Gollywhoppers

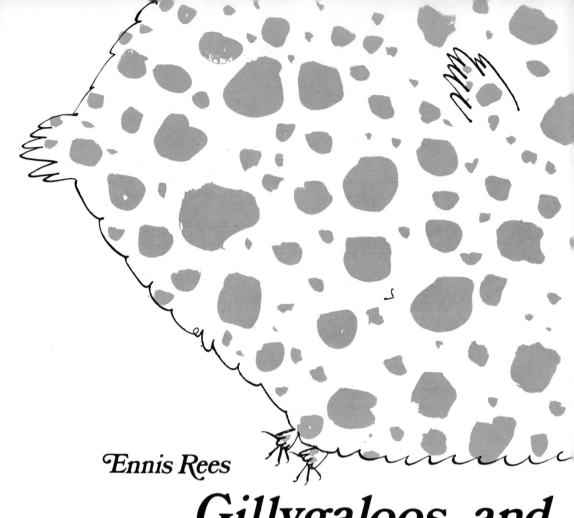

Ennis Rees

Gillygaloos and

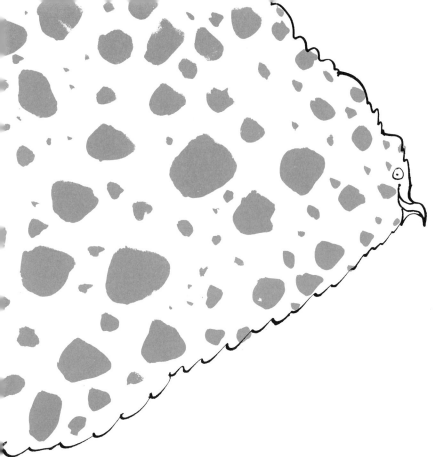

Tall Tales about Mythical Monsters

Gollywhoppers

Illustrated by *Quentin Blake*

Abelard-Schuman LONDON NEW YORK TORONTO

LONDON
Abelard-Schuman
Limited
8 King St. WC2

NEW YORK
Abelard-Schuman
Limited
6 West 57th St.

TORONTO
Abelard-Schuman
Canada Limited
1680 Midland Ave.

note

*

Almost any early mythology will yield its share of fabulous creatures such as Homer's Chimaera (lion's head, serpent's tail, goat's body) and Scylla (twelve feet, six long necks, and heads with triple tiers of teeth). Dreams are also a well-known source of chimerical creatures. But the monsters of dreams and early mythologies are seldom very funny. What distinguishes the American tall tale is that it almost always is (and most of the creatures in the rhymes of this book are) part of America's tall-tale lore. Their names alone will often conjure up creature enough — the Roperite, the Flitterick, the Tote-Road Shagamaw, the Tripodero, the Mouthless Dingmaul, the Saucer-Back Halibut, the Moogie Bird. To wanderers and farmers in the American wilderness, the impulse to tell of the No-Neck Wunk recently encountered in the wilds of Arkansas or Michigan was irresistible — or, if not the Wunk, the Linkum-sluice, the Treesqueak, the Luferlang, the Hinge-Tailed Bing-buffer, and many others, including the Squonk and the Cross-Feathered Snee, to say nothing of the extremely rare Teakettler and Snazzy.

E. R.

The Gillygaloo is an earnest bird
   That does its level best.
It lays square eggs in order to keep them
   From rolling out of the nest.

The Gollywhopper is so big
　Its eggs weigh almost a ton.
Whenever it flies across the sky
　It completely blots out the sun.

The Snoligoster is a beast
   That looks like the Side-Hill Dodger,
Except its legs are the same on both sides
   And its dodging-holes much larger.

*

The Flitterick is a flying squirrel
   Of a kind you almost never see.
In flight it is invisible
   It flies with such rapidity.

*

The Billdad catches many fish.
   Its method cannot fail.
It dives hawklike upon a pond
   And stuns them with its tail.

The Ogre Rabbit runs the dogs
  Till they are out of breath,
Then jumps at them from behind a tree
  And scares them half to death.

Bed Cats are in reality bugs,
    But the cowboys call them that
Because when they find one in their beds
    It's always big as a cat!

*

The Pinnacle Grouse has only one wing
    And a kind of corkscrew bill.
It can fly rings around anything,
    But prefers the top of a hill.

*

The Toodalong Fish has long blonde hair
  And a great big flukey tail.
When it's seen from a distance, sailors swear
  It's a mermaid riding a whale.

*

The Rinctum Rhino rests itself
  By leaning its bulk against a tree.
Since it has no joints, if you cut the tree down
  The creature's as helpless as can be.

*

The Mouthless Dingmaul, or Pounding Plunkus,
  Has hammer-heads for toes.
It pounds its victim into a gas,
  Then inhales it through its nose.

The only protection against the Hodag
   Is something sour, like a lemon.
If you don't have a lemon to squirt him with,
   Try a green persimmon.

*

It's hard for the Saucer-Back Halibut
    To find enough water to float in.
Its saucer alone is big enough
    For a man to sail a boat in!

*

So agile is the Linkumsluice
    You never really find him.
No matter how quickly his victim spins,
    The Linkumsluice stays behind him.

*

The Vain Pomola is a beast
    Of many foolish deeds.
It knots its tail around its neck
    And pretends it's wearing beads

The Teakettler is a brown little beast,
  Though sometimes there's a green one.
White whistling steam comes from its snout.
  Some people have never seen one.

*

The Tote-Road Shagamaw's hind legs
  Have the hooves of a big bull moose.
Its front legs end in the claws of a bear,
  But it's harmless as a goose.

Its diet consists of woolen clothes
  And the hair of sheep and goats.
It wanders the tote-roads looking for
  Jackets and sweaters and coats.

*

The Waw-Waw Fish is half as big
  As any normal ocean,
But it almost never moves at all,
  Since it just has "half a notion."

*

The No-Neck Wunk looks like a stove
  And is blamed for many forest fires.
It can change its coat from black to red
  Whenever it so desires.

In the fall the Wympsis covers itself
   From head to tail with resin and pitch,
Then rolls on the ground till it's covered with
    leaves,
   Which keep it warm—but they itch!

*

To catch the Swelling Wendigo
   Two things you must make:
An ugly face and, worse than that,
   A square hole in the lake.

Then when this fish sticks out its head
   You make a face like a troll,
Whereat it swells with rage until
   It can't get back down the hole.

*

The Whiffenpoofit is a fish
   That's very seldom found,
For the only lakes the fish can live in
   Are those that are perfectly round.

*

The rare Orance has two sets of legs
   But is captured without a chase,
For it tries to run both ways at once
   And stays in the very same place.

The Phillyloo Bird looks like a crane
But has even longer legs.
Since it has no knees, it can't sit down,
So it lays only broken eggs.

*

One of the most amazing beasts
   Is the Geek-Squaw Hide-Behind,
But because it's always in back of a tree
   It's impossible to find.

*

The Luferlang bites once a year
   And after that will not attack.
It has a big umbrella tail
   That grows from the middle of its back.

*

The Hugag is the biggest beast,
   So big that everywhere
You see those leaning trees you know
   What leaned against them there.

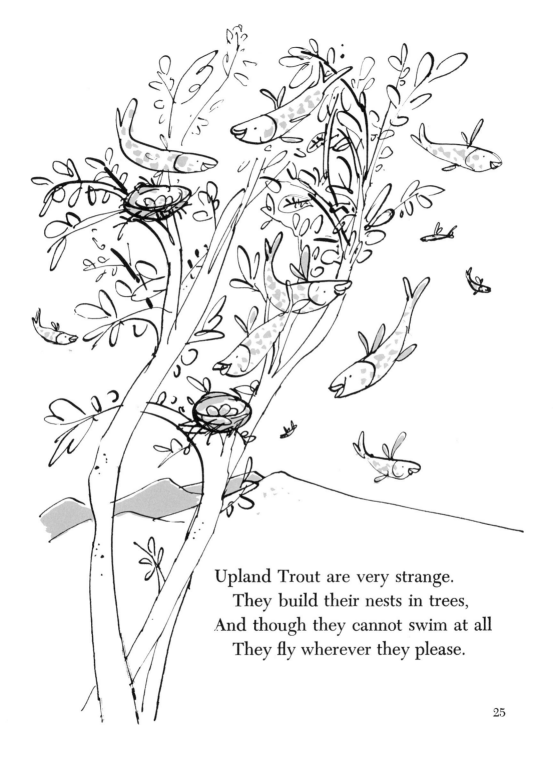

Upland Trout are very strange.
They build their nests in trees,
And though they cannot swim at all
They fly wherever they please.

25

Few have seen a Treesqueak,
  But many have heard its call.
Sometimes it's a whine, sometimes a shriek,
  Sometimes a caterwaul.

The Squonk's a very bashful beast,
    Haunted by its fears.
When cornered in the woods it may
    Dissolve itself in tears.

The Cactus Cat has a knifelike tail
    And yards of thorny hair.
If you ever hear its hungry wail
    You'd better get out of there!

For hunting the Timberdoodle
  A mirror is a must.
One look at itself and the Timberdoodle
  Collapses in disgust.

＊

Why the Guffel Bird flies backward
  No one understands.
Some think it's because he's a contrary bird
  And doesn't care where he lands.

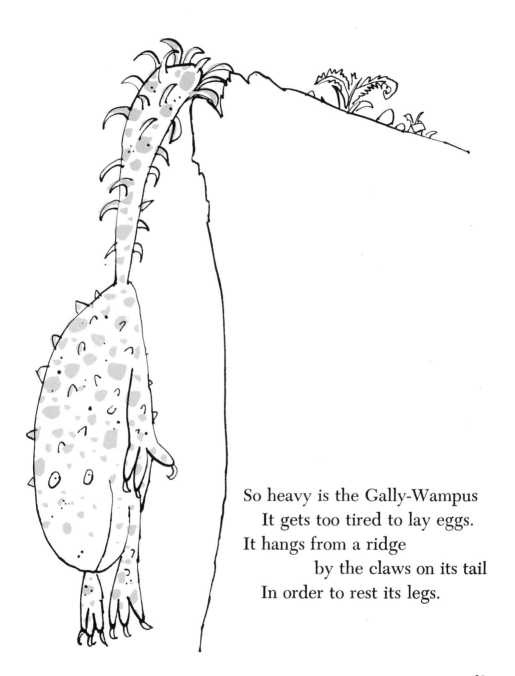

So heavy is the Gally-Wampus
 It gets too tired to lay eggs.
It hangs from a ridge
  by the claws on its tail
In order to rest its legs.

*

The Milermore Bird is a whistler
And you can hear it just fine
When it blows reveille at 5 A.M.
Or the curfew nightly at nine.

*

The Whirling Wimpus spins about
And makes a droning sound,
And also it's invisible,
So fast it whirls around.

Whatever it strikes with its paddle paws
Is jellied for its food,
Since jelly is all its stomach can stand—
A dizzy beast but shrewd!

The Auger Fish has a corkscrew snout
    With which it bores holes in boats.
It turns so fast it can bore a hole
    In anything that floats.

The Whiffle Bird flies backward,
  Not because of its size,
But to keep the bothersome dust
  Out of its beautiful eyes.

The Come-at-a-Body is frightening
  When it rushes at you ZOOM!
But all it does is stop and grin,
  Then spray you with perfume.

The Snow Wasset sheds its legs
  And slides about in the snow.
It's amazing to see how rapidly
  The Snow Wasset can go.

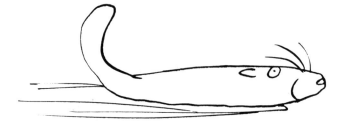

The Yamhill Prock has so many legs
  It's very hard to beat.
Whenever the bottom four get tired,
  It runs on four other feet.

*

One look at the poisonous Darby-Hick
   Will irritate your eyes.
Whenever a Darby-Hick bites a log
   It swells to twice its size.

*

The Snawfus is a monstrous deer
   No hunter ever kills.
The breath it snorts out on the air
   Is the blue haze over the hills.

*

At the foot of Big Hog Mountain
   Lies the hungry Big Hog Bear.
When the pigs get so fat they roll downhill,
   He's waiting for them there!

The Splinter Cat, in search of fun,
  Dives from tree to tree,
And everyone it dives upon
  Is splintered totally.

The Moskitto Bird is an insect,
　　But the loggers say it's absurd
To call it a blooming insect
　　When it's really big as a bird!

The Whopperknocker can't be shot,
  Nor does it have to run.
It can see so well it ducks the bullet
  Before it leaves the gun!

*

The Devil Jack Blue-Diamond Fish
  Has scales of steel as blue as the sky.
Whenever it strikes a piece of flint,
  You can see the little sparks fly!

*

When the Hinge-Tailed Bingbuffer spots its prey
    It takes a stone from its pouch
And hurls it so hard with its long flat tail
    There's seldom time to say "Ouch!"

*

The Augerino is a worm
    That looks like a great big drill.
It can let the water from ditches and lakes
    Or tunnel through a hill.

*

When the people had paid to see the Sky Foogle,
    The crook who'd collected would yell,
"Run for your lives! The Foogle's loose!"
    And the people would run pell-mell.

The Rumptifusel is all fur,
   Blanket-size and very thin.
Woodsmen who think it's a new fur coat
   Are lost and missing men.

The Whirlygig Fish are caught in the winter
    Through holes smeared with ham till they smell
        very nice.
The fish swim so fast around these holes
    They whirl themselves out on the ice.

*

The Fur-Bearing Trout has tiny claws
  And fur like the Spiral Mango-Bat's.
It's short and a kind of silver-blue
  Much finer than a cat's.

*

The Catawampus has an arm
  That folds or shoots up high.
He uses it for plucking turkeys
  And eagles from the sky.

Sometimes instead of a turkey or eagle
  He catches a Turkeagle—well,
He doesn't really know the difference,
  Since he cannot spell!

*

The Wowzer's a panther that lives down South
  And is so incredibly big
It can jump a fence with a steer in its mouth
  Or swallow a full-grown pig.

The Ponjureen flies upside-down
   And its nest is turned over and all awry.
If from the nest an egg escapes
   It quickly rises toward the sky.

*

An Egress isn't an animal
   Of the sort that walks on all fours.
It's something that you walk through yourself
   Into all out-of-doors.

The Agropelter lives in trees,
Up high in the hollow trunks.
From there it pelts its victims with
Splinters of wood and chunks.

43

The Tripodero has tripod legs
  And a snout that looks like a gun.
When it tires of hunting for its prey
  It target-shoots for fun.

*

The purple eggs of the Willipus-Wallipus
   Are three and a half feet long.
People break them with a hammer,
   But some say they taste a bit strong.

*

The Snazzy has scales on only one side
   And it's a very flat fish.
On the other side it has nothing but hide,
   Sort of like that on a catfish.

*

The Moogie Bird is so enormous
   That when it flies around
Its great black shadow wears a trail
   In even the hardest ground.

The Log Gar is an enormous fish
  With teeth that nothing can stop.
It quickly saws through the biggest log
  To get at the man on top.

＊

The Bouncer Fish is easily caught
  And you can catch them galore
By quickly hitting each fish with a paddle
  And letting them bounce up on shore.

＊

The Goofang Fish swims backward,
  Or at least the poor thing tries,
For that's the only way it can keep
  The water out of its eyes.

＊

The Cross-Feathered Snee, to my surprise,
  Is seldom seen here lately.
Two beams of light shine from its eyes
  And it winks them alternately.

*

The Sand-Bar Fish is a monstrous fish
   And never has been landed.
On its back it carries tons of sand
   And when a ship strikes it, it's stranded!

*

      The Snow Snake's bite is a fatal bite,
         And few snakes are so mean.
      But it lives far north and is snow white,
         So it's almost never seen.

*

The Panther Fish is a savage fish
   With awesome claws and teeth.
It reaches up and grabs a logger
   And jerks him underneath.

The Jimplicute feeds on nothing but stones
And it lays big hard-boiled eggs.
It easily feeds on the sides of hills
Since it has adjustable legs.

*

The Rod-and-Reel Snake, if held by the tail,
Is as useful as you could wish,
For he plunges his head down into the water
And quickly comes up with a fish!

*

The Trout-Catching Deer impales the trout
Upon his antler tips,
Then holds them over a fire to broil
While loudly smacking his lips.

*

The Financial Fish Hound dives after quarters
And comes up looking strange,
For in his mouth he brings a catfish
And fifteen cents in change.

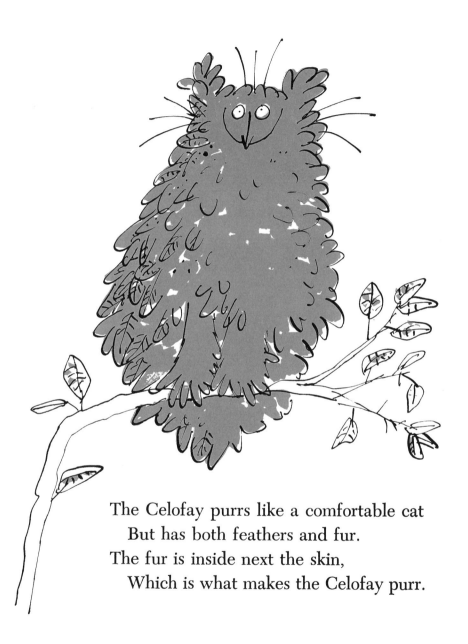

The Celofay purrs like a comfortable cat
    But has both feathers and fur.
The fur is inside next the skin,
    Which is what makes the Celofay purr.

*

The Clothesline Snake comes up in the yard
   And stretches itself between
The clothesline poles, where it hangs on hard.
   It's long and very lean!

*

Born in the mountains, the Terrashot
   When grown comes down the mountain roads,
Then walks the desert until it's so hot
   The boiling beast explodes!

*

The best of all climbers is the Wapaloosie
   With long cat-claws and a spike on its tail.
It humps up a tree like a measuring worm,
   And there's nothing it cannot scale.

Instead of a beak the Roperite
   Has a noose with which it ropes
Unwary dogs and lumberjacks
   And the swiftest antelopes.

The Sliver Cat's tail is very long
  And ends in a heavy ball.
It swings this weapon from a limb
  And WHAM! its victims fall.

*

The Slide-Rock Bolter lives in the mountains
And hangs with its head down a slope.
Then it slides down the rocks and scoops up
the tourists.
Do any escape it? Nope!

*

To catch a Whiffle-Poofle
You must find a water spout,
Then bore a deep hole in the water
And wait till one comes out.

*

A travelling Club-Tailed Glyptodont
Would make 'most anyone smile.
It uses its big stiff rubbery tail
To bounce along Pogo style.

When all the men are sound asleep
   And out are their lanterns and candles,
The Axhandle Hound sneaks into camp
   And eats up all their ax-handles.

A beast that lives till it explodes
   Is the Leathery Gumberoo.
A foolish man once photographed one,
   But the picture blew up, too.

The Sand Squink is an animal
  That every woodsman fears,
For it feeds on nothing but electric eels
  Which highly charge its ears.

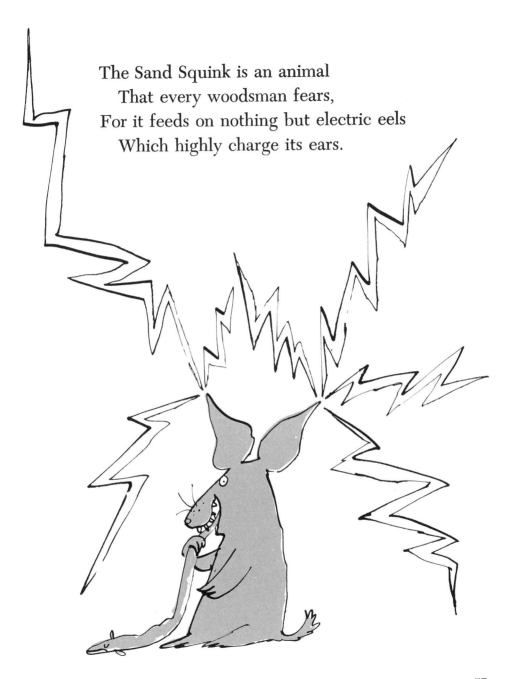

*

The Flying Hawk-Fish leaves the water
  And flies up to attack
A turkey or an eagle, and always
  Brings one back.

*

The Vampire Mosquito feeds on the stock
  But seldom gets its fill.
Under one wing it carries a rock
  Which it uses to sharpen its bill.

*

The Dog Mosquito of Mexico,
  As soon as it gets dark,
Comes out with its litter of puppy mosquitoes
  To light on the trees and bark.

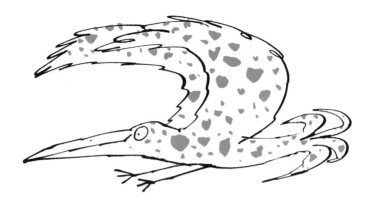

The Bogie Bird flies backward
  But only at those times when
It doesn't care where it's going
  But wants to see where it's been.

The Hoop Snake puts its tail in its mouth
    And rapidly rolls at its prey.
To escape you have to jump through the hoop,
    And that's the only way.

One famous thing about the Hoop Snake
    May seem a little tall,
But they say it can swallow itself until
    There is nothing left at all.

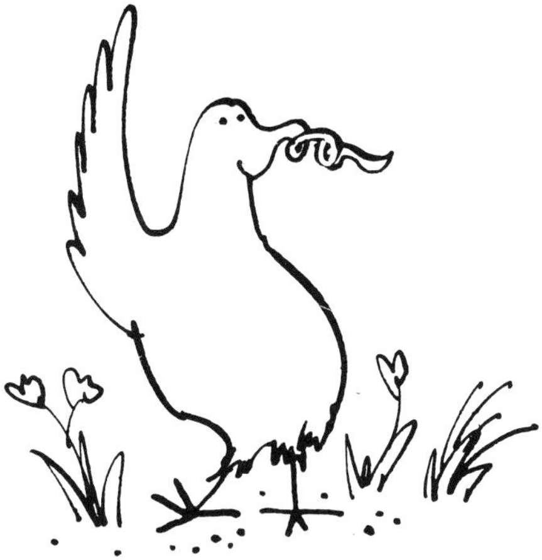